Original title:
The Oak's Epilogue

Copyright © 2025 Creative Arts Management OÜ
All rights reserved.

Author: Penelope Hawthorne
ISBN HARDBACK: 978-1-80567-053-7
ISBN PAPERBACK: 978-1-80567-133-6

Beneath the Canopy's Embrace

Squirrels dance with acorn hats,
While birds critique the fashion stats.
A crow tells jokes, he's quite the wit,
While rabbits giggle, won't admit.

The sun peeks through, all in a glow,
Leaves whisper secrets, just so-so.
The breeze brings laughter, a silly tune,
As butterflies flutter, making a swoon.

Tales Woven in Bark

Once a tree stood tall and proud,
Now it tells tales, spoken loud.
In knots and rings, great stories spun,
Of silly raccoons who thought they could run.

A woodpecker laughed at a pigeon's strut,
While ants in line played follow the nut.
Under the boughs, life dances and twirls,
Where flowers gossip and laughter unfurls.

Shadows of Time Underneath

In shadows deep, the critters play,
Dreaming up games through the day.
A turtle jokes, 'I'll race you across!'
But the hare just smiles, knowing he's at a loss.

Stumps become seats for grandiose talks,
While fireflies glow like tiny clocks.
Laughter echoes, a symphony bright,
In the wild wonder, all feels just right.

The Final Leaves Descend

As leaves drop down, they spin and swirl,
The squirrels dive in, what a wild whirl!
Old branches creak with a chuckle deep,
While the ground below hides treasures to keep.

A wise old owl hoots, "What's happened here?"
The answer comes squeaky, "Autumn is near!"
With every fall, new laughter begins,
As nature rejoices in playful spins.

The Legacy of Gnarled Boughs

In a forest where squirrels debate,
A gnarled old tree decided its fate.
"I'll grow a few branches, so grand and spry,
To catch all the birds that just zoom by!"

Its bark was quite wrinkly, and twisted with style,
With a wink and a nod, it added a smile.
"I'm wise beyond years, yet still like to play,
Who says trees can't joke at the end of the day?"

Upon the Boughs of Time

Upon boughs of time, a wise owl took flight,
He chuckled at branches swaying left and right.
"Hey, tree, let's have a dance, if you're game!
I promise I'll leave you unharmed, just the same!"

The tree shook its leaves, all rustling squeaks,
"I can't jump or twirl, but I sure can creak!
Let's sway and have fun till the sun starts to set,
And remember this dance, there's no need to fret!"

Where Acorns Dream in Slumber

Where acorns dream, under stars so bright,
They dream of adventures that spark sheer delight.
"Let's roll down the hill, it'll be such a blast!
We'll race to the bottom, no time for the past!"

But one sleepy acorn just yawned and said,
"I'm staying right here, on my cozy bed!
You squirrels can have all the wild, crazy fun,
I'll just dream of snacks 'til the morning sun!"

The Chronicle of Weathered Wood

In a book of old tales, where wood stories dwell,
A tree claimed it knew every secret and spell.
"I've seen lovers carve hearts, in bark that won't fade,
And kids climb my limbs till their plans are all made!"

"But the best of my tales are the ones that we share,
Like the time that a bear tried to climb with flair!
He slipped, and he tumbled, with a great, funny puff,
Now he's called 'Clumsy'—couldn't get enough!"

The Keeper of Nature's Secrets

In the hollow of a tree, a squirrel's party,
With acorn hats and laughter so hearty.
They dance on branches like it's a show,
While whispers of wind join the row.

Old Badger, the judge, claps his paws loud,
Declaring a nutty king for the crowd.
With tiny crowns made of twigs they proclaim,
For nature's secrets, they play a fun game.

Beside a Rooted History

Beneath the old branches, tales intertwine,
Of trees dressed in moss with a glass of wine.
They gossip of squirrels who hoard and forget,
And giggle at rabbits who trip on a bet.

The wise old owl spins yarns full of cheer,
About trees that dance when humans aren't near.
Every root holds a story, a riddle to share,
To make you chuckle, toss back your hair.

Chronicles of the Leafless Winter

In winter's grasp, the branches are bare,
But snowflakes sparkle with comedic flair.
A rabbit in mittens hops by with a grin,
Claiming he's winning at not getting thin.

Icicles dangle like nature's sharp swords,
While birds gossip freely in humorous chords.
As frost forms on boughs in a bizarre ballet,
The trees hold their breath, watching the play.

Breeze upon the Broken Trunk

A windy day blew a tree half away,
But still, it found humor in nature's foray.
With half of a trunk and a crooked old smile,
It hosted a gathering, full of style.

The creatures all came with their quirkiest tales,
Of nuts that went missing and thunderous gales.
The trunk swayed and chuckled, defying all pain,
While laughter danced wildly like drops in the rain.

Echoes Beneath the Canopy

In a tree that stands so tall,
Squirrels host their nutty ball.
Acorns drop like tiny bombs,
While raccoons sing their funny psalms.

Branches shake in breezy glee,
'Why's that groundhog laughing at me?'
With each gust, a giggle flies,
Nature's jest beneath the skies.

Mushrooms pop like party hats,
As bugs dance in crazy spats.
Leaves rustle in a whispered joke,
'Who's the best? The sun or oak?'

Laughter echoes, roots entwine,
In this comedy divine.
While shadows frolic on the floor,
Nature's stage, forevermore.

A Tapestry of Seasons Gone

Autumn leaves in colors bright,
A fashion show—what sheer delight!
Each gust a runway, crisp and loud,
While critters strut, immensely proud.

Winter whispers, snowflakes cheer,
'Oh look, a snowman's growing here!'
With carrots stuck for noses proud,
A frosty grin that gathers crowds.

Springtime hops with bouncy flair,
Every bloom a fresh affair.
'Watch me grow!' the flowers shout,
While bees buzz, making rounds about.

Summer frolics, sun on high,
The treehouse swings and children fly.
With laughter ringing, joy is spun,
A tapestry of endless fun.

Twilight Among the Timber

In twilight's glow, the shadows play,
As owls hoot jokes they share all day.
The crickets chirp with rhythm tight,
While fireflies twinkle, pure delight.

'Who's the king of the forest floor?'
A raccoon laughs, 'I just adore!'
While deer prance in their graceful way,
'We've got the moves, come join the fray!'

Mice pop out for a late-night chat,
'What's the latest gossip? Oh, that!'
The wind joins in with a playful breeze,
Tickling branches, rustling leaves.

Twilight's stage, the stars come out,
As treetops whisper, laugh and shout.
Nature's dance beneath the sun,
In this forest, laughter's never done.

Shadows of the Stalwart

Beneath strong limbs, the shadows laugh,
    As sunlight sketches a funny path.
    The roots below hold tales untold,
Of wise old whispers and mischief bold.

'What's that rumbling in the dark?'
A raccoon grins, 'Just me, no spark!'
With shadows stretching, fun they weave,
    As creatures gather, none believe.

Mushrooms giggle, sprouting wide,
    'Jump on us! Come take a ride!'
While toads croak riddles, quite absurd,
    In this woodland, joy's inferred.

As dusk descends, the laughter stays,
    In every leaf, in every blaze.
    Shadows play, and spirits soar,
In the heart of woods, we laugh once more.

Footsteps in the Fallen Leaves

Crunchy sounds beneath my feet,
Squirrels dance to a nutty beat.
Each step a joke the trees will tell,
As foliage laughs, oh can't you smell?

I trip on roots, oh what a sight!
Leaves scatter, taking flight at night.
A grand adventure, or so it seems,
In nature's playground, bursting with dreams.

A leafy carpet, thick and bright,
Whispers of mischief, oh what a fright!
But I stomp louder with silly glee,
While squirrels giggle up in the tree.

So if you wander through this maze,
Watch your step and count the ways.
Nature's humor tucked in each fold,
In every leaf, a story's told.

The Stillness of an Aged Canopy

Beneath the branches, time does pause,
In stillness hangs a squirrel's cause.
Gnarled limbs creak with whispered fables,
Of treehouse dreams and picnic tables.

A bark so rough, it's like a mask,
Holding secrets, if you dare to ask.
But who can hear through the old oak's sigh?
Maybe that crow who's flying high.

Lichens chatter like old friends,
Gossiping about where the sun bends.
And if you listen very close,
You'll hear their laughter, a soft, sweet boast.

So stroll beneath this aged shield,
Where nature's wisdom is revealed.
Each rustle and shake, a joke so fine,
In the stillness, the punchlines shine.

Embracing the Passage of Time

Time flows like sap, slow and sticky,
Yet humor hides in every tricksy.
From leaf to leaf and ring to ring,
The old tree chuckles at everything.

Seasons pass, in an endless loop,
Winter's chill brings a funny swoop.
A snowy hat on branches wide,
Laughter echoes where the squirrels hide.

Buds break forth, like jokes in spring,
With flowers blooming, oh what a fling!
Nature's jesters dressed in bright hues,
Dancing on breezes, sharing their views.

So let's toast to the passing years,
With laughter, joy, and a few cute tears.
Life's a jest as we sway and climb,
A funny tale embracing time.

Against the Whispering Wind

Windy day, oh what a tease,
Whispers secrets through the trees.
Branches sway, a dance they share,
Tickling leaves with gentle care.

Each gust brings tales from afar,
Of acorns dreaming of being a star.
But don't be fooled by their soft sigh,
They plot and scheme as clouds roll by.

Feathered friends join in the fun,
Chirping jokes while on the run.
The breeze carries laughter, round and round,
Echoes of joy in nature's sound.

So let the wind be our guide,
In its laughter, we must abide.
For even trees must learn to grin,
Against the whispers, let joy begin.

The Weight of Years on a Single Limb

A branch that bends, oh how it creaks,
It squeaks like me when I try to speak.
With wisdom stuck, stuck in the grooves,
It's hard to dance when you've got the moves.

The squirrels laugh like they know the score,
They leap around, I just want to snore.
Each twig a tale of splinters and spring,
Yet here I sway, and I still can't sing.

The sunbeams tickle my weary frame,
While I ponder if it's all just a game.
These leaves have seen my youthful days,
Now they add a touch of gray in the rays.

So raise a glass, don't start to pout,
For wisdom gained is what it's about.
In all my weight, I'm light as a dream,
Join me, dear friend, let's sip on that cream.

In the Wake of the Fallen

Branches scatter, like confetti in air,
A party of leaves, slightly beyond repair.
Once they waved like kids with a prize,
Now they lie low, hiding from the skies.

One leaf whispered, "I used to be bright!"
But now it's brown, trying to take flight.
The wind chuckles; what a messy affair,
"Time to rake up! Who's got time to care?"

From heights of glory, to earth beneath,
Where squirrels plan their nutty grief.
They scatter tales of ages gone by,
As I stand tall, watching the sky.

So gather round, let's celebrate loss,
With cider and jokes, we'll be our own boss.
In every rustle, there's laughter too,
As we toast the fallen, old friends and new.

Parables of the Ancient Canopy

In a forest vast, where tales intertwine,
The squirrels play judge, with acorns divine.
"Who's the wisest?" they chatter with glee,
But I've seen them trip on the roots, oh me!

I share my wisdom in leaves that flutter,
They hear my tales but just roll in the gutter.
"Don't climb too high," I whisper and sigh,
Then watch them leap again, daring the sky.

A woodpecker knocks, a brisk, clever rap,
He's always in search of the latest flap.
"Need lessons in patience?" I shout with a grin,
But he's off for a snack—what a bold little kin!

In the canopy's shade, as shadows grow long,
We share a laugh over fresh branches gone wrong.
For wisdom can wait, like seeds in the ground,
And in every rustle, our joys can be found.

Quiet Farewells in the Thicket

As dusk approaches, we gather in bunches,
With whispers of leaves and some clumsy crunches.
A bee buzzes by, it's not saying bye,
Just drunk on the nectar under the sky.

Old branches mutter, "It's time for repose,"
While the wind plays soft tunes, teasing my prose.
I bid goodbye to the stars above,
In this thicket of whispers, we still find love.

The shadows grow longer, as critters scurry,
With laughter that echoes, yet there's not a hurry.
The moon lends a wink, casting soft, silver light,
Guiding us gently into the night.

So let's raise a cheer for the moments we keep,
In a world of wonders, both wide and steep.
With quiet farewells and tales spun anew,
I'll hold you close, my friends, in the dew.

Beneath the Weight of Wrinkled Leaves

In autumn's glow, the branches sigh,
Leaves tumble down like a clumsy pie.
Squirrels dash, thinking it's their parade,
While gravity laughs, it's nature's charade.

Each leaf has stories, gossip from the past,
Whispers of critters and a wind so vast.
One leaf shouts loudly, 'I used to be green!'
But now he just giggles, 'Look at me, I'm seen!'

Time's Reverie in Knotted Roots

Roots tangled together, a jumbled affair,
They argue at night, who's got more flair.
One thinks he's wiser, like a sage from the woods,
The other just chuckles, 'I've got all the goods!'

In the shadowed depths, they swap funny tales,
Of raccoons with dreams of setting their sails.
While beetles run races, and worms tell their jokes,
The roots just roll over, snorting with hoaxes.

Protector of the Woodland Realm

A guardian stands with a bark like a shield,
Watching the antics of the woodland yield.
Rabbits hold council, in their fluffy attire,
While owls chuckle softly, like a post-office choir.

The hedgehogs debate on who's rolled the best ball,
And frogs throw a dance party—what a silly sprawl!
They know their protector has seen it all play,
As he chuckles and sighs, 'What'll happen today?'

In the Stillness of Solstice

When solstice arrives, there's a giggle in air,
The sun wears a cap with a festive flair.
Critters unite for a grand evening show,
As fireflies waltz with a flickering glow.

The moon cracks a joke, makes the shadows laugh,
While squirrels stumble, trying to take a cool half.
Nature's a party, no worries in line,
In the still of the night, everything's fine.

Autumn's Last Farewell

Leaves are dancing, what a sight,
Falling down in pure delight.
Squirrels claiming all their loot,
Avoiding acorns as they scoot.

Wind takes selfies, trees in pose,
Nature's runway, striking shows.
Acorns giggle as they drop,
"Watch your step!" they seem to hop.

Birds are laughing, passing by,
"More cozy nests, oh me, oh my!"
Chubby pumpkins wear a grin,
As harvest feasts begin to spin.

With a wink, the sun retreats,
Ending parties, fun-filled feats.
Autumn chuckles, takes a bow,
"See you next time—I'm outta now!"

Guardians of the Forest Heart

In the woods, the guardians play,
Squirrels plotting their buffet.
Rabbits gossip 'neath the moon,
Each secret shared, they hoot and swoon.

Badgers dance with rhythmic flair,
Wielding sticks, banishing despair.
Owls hoot jokes that reach the stars,
While fireflies flash their secret bars.

Fungi brigade rolls with the beat,
In wild uniforms, they can't be beat.
They run a shop of mushroom hats,
With signs that say, "Tippy-tap chats!"

The forest thrives with giggles loud,
From trees that sway, they're oh so proud.
With every rustle, every cheer,
The heart of nature holds them near.

The Resilient Whisperer

Beneath the boughs, a whisper flows,
Telling tales that no one knows.
Nature's secrets, wrapped in jest,
Leaves chuckle softly, feeling blessed.

The wind's a prankster, full of glee,
Shaking branches, "Dance with me!"
Squirrels roll in laughter's spree,
As nature's jesters roam so free.

Raccoons plot their late-night feasts,
"Who will win?" as hunger crests.
Branches sway with every prank,
Creating smiles by riverbank.

Even the stones chuckle and grin,
As laughter echoes from within.
Whispers and giggles fill the night,
In the forest, everything feels right.

Legacy of the Twisted Trunk

Twisted trunk with stories spun,
Holds the laughter of the sun.
Branches sway like old folks dance,
In a spiraled, joyful prance.

Knots and turns, a silly sight,
Echoing joy from morning light.
Roots that tangle, seek their friends,
In a maze where humor bends.

Animals gather, hear the tales,
Of a trunk that sings and wails.
"Oops! There goes another branch!"
With every laugh, they start to prance.

In this legacy, joy unfolds,
As each new story warmly holds.
Twisted trees, with funny flair,
Breathe in laughter, anywhere.

Keepers of the Woodland Secrets

In the heart of the woods, a squirrel's plight,
Hiding nuts like treasures, till the frosty night.
Whispers of secrets from the branches high,
Where acorns mock passers with a cheeky sigh.

The wise old owl hoots, 'Who's in for a jest?'
While raccoons plan mischief, at their fuzzy best.
Frogs croak in laughter, toads roll on the ground,
As the trees share tales, that echo all around.

A hedgehog's stuck fast, with his prickly pride,
While the fox prances 'round, acting oh-so-wide.
The woods are a circus, with nature's own fun,
Where the sun sets in giggles, as day is done.

So come join the party, where laughter is free,
With critters confiding beneath every tree.
For secrets kept cozy are treasures to tease,
In the realms of the woodland, so full of glee.

The Dance of Ageing Limbs

When roots take a shuffle and branches sway,
Old trees throw a party at the end of the day.
With a creak and a groan, they begin to groove,
Flickering leaves in an age-old move.

Barks wrinkle with laughter, twigs twist with cheer,
The forest floor echoes, 'The dance is right here!'
As the wind joins the jig, in a whimsical whir,
Even the mushrooms join in, with a curious stir.

A grandpa tree chuckles, 'Watch my trunk take flight!'
While the younger saplings giggle, oh what a sight!
They all sway together, in a whimsical trance,
For even the old ones deserve a good dance.

So here's to the greenery, and wisdom in boughs,
Where laughter grows louder, and joy makes a vow.
In the dance of the ages, with roots deep in ground,
The trees keep on twirling, together they're bound.

An Ode to Decaying Glory

A tree once so mighty, now tired and gray,
With branches like fans, that sway day by day.
It stands as a throne, for bugs of all sorts,
Hosting raucous debates, in nature's courts.

Fungi wear hats as they march up the trunk,
While ants wield their swords, in a line, all in funk.
The bark cracks a joke, with a twiggy old jest,
As leaves fall like confetti, in a seasonal fest.

The crows caw with glee, perched high on their perch,
Sipping afternoon tea, with a fine leafy birch.
While the wind plays the music, of old golden dreams,
The glory of ages, or so it seems.

So here's to the bump, the twist, and the bend,
To all of the trees that continue to trend.
Though glory may fade, and glory may dwindle,
The laughter remains, like a sweet forest swindle.

Canvas of Seasons Past

Once a painter of green, now a splash of bright gold,
Leaves litter the ground, tales waiting to be told.
A canvas of seasons, each brushstroke a tale,
From winter's cold grip, to summer's warm hail.

Sprites jump through puddles, while birds laugh and sing,

As colors collide like a whimsical fling.
The trees wear their scars, like badges of play,
In the rich, quiet woods, where mischief holds sway.

The autumn leaves giggle as they spiral and dance,
While squirrels race under, in a nut-finding trance.
Every twist, every turn, is a laugh in disguise,
As the seasons like jesters, perform 'neath the skies.

So paint me a mural with laughter and light,
A tapestry woven, from morning to night.
For in every rustle, and every bright hue,
The symphony's funny, forever anew.

Whispers of Ancient Branches

In the heart of the grove, whispers dance,
Leaves gossiping secrets, given a chance.
Squirrels debate with a jolly old crow,
"Who wears the best acorn? Now, that's quite a show!"

Under the shade, the shadows conspire,
Branches creak softly, adding to the choir.
The termites are plotting a small ceiling coup,
While the owls hold court—who knew they could stew?

Rabbits hop by, with a curious stare,
Wondering aloud if there's food hidden there.
A wise old raccoon with a blink and a grin,
Says, "Join the fun, let the games just begin!"

With roots intertwined in a goofy embrace,
Nature's own comedians, out to chase space.
In laughter they linger, through daylight's soft glow,
These ancient old branches—what a lively show!

Last Leaves of Autumn's Breath

The last leaves waltz, in a whirlwind of cheer,
Twirling and twisting, drawing friends near.
Blustery breezes, with a tickle and tease,
"Catch me if you can!" they call with such ease.

Squirrels in sweaters, so bold and so bright,
Scurry and hop, what a comical sight!
They stash acorns with such fervent delight,
Forgetful, they pause, "Was that my last bite?"

The mushrooms laugh, silent in shades of brown,
Giggling softly, they peek from the ground.
Chasing their shadows, the critters all play,
In this leafy circus, autumn's grand finalé.

As the sun dips low, painting skies with a grin,
These jesters of nature, let the fun begin!
With laughter and joy, they wave their farewell,
In rustles and whispers, oh what tales to tell!

The Silent Sentinel's Farewell

A tree stood tall, with a wink in its bark,
Witness to secrets, a favorite landmark.
With a giggle of sap and a twist of a leaf,
It chuckled at birds who claimed to be chief.

"Cracks in my bark? It's called character, friends!"
Said the sentinel wise, "My fun never ends!"
Raccoons playing poker with moonlight above,
Peeking from nests in a raucous of love.

Among branches so sturdy, the whispers collide,
Gossipy owls, with a shimmer of pride.
"Did you hear what they said? The winds' such a hoot!"
The leaves trembled softly, "Oh, what truth in the fruit!"

And with every goodbye, the laughter would swell,
As the sun dipped low to bid its own farewell.
"Catch me on the breeze!" the wise branches did call,
In the heart of the forest, they'd always stand tall!

Roots in Time's Embrace

With roots intertwined, like a grand old parade,
The stories they share are simply displayed.
"Who spilled the pollen? Was it me or the bee?"
Laughter erupts from the roots of the tree.

Time whispers softly through leaves in a rush,
With a rustle and giggle, it turns into hush.
The beetles confer on their glowing award,
"Best in the garden, you'll never be bored!"

As evening descends, the crickets start play,
In a symphony pitch where they frolic and sway.
"Shall we dance with the glowworms? A flash of delight!"
The roots roll their eyes, "Let's party all night!"

In the embrace of the earth, a very fine crew,
Each twist and each turn, brings fresh laughter anew.
Together they sit, in this playful ballet,
Roots in a rapture, come join in the fray!

Reflections in the Woodland

In a forest so grand, where the sunlight beams,
Squirrels plot mischief and share their dreams.
A chipmunk once claimed he could outsmart a crow,
But he slipped on a nut and fell flat, oh no!

The wise old owl chuckled from high in his nest,
While raccoons debated who looked the best.
They donned little masks, a fashion parade,
But tripped on their tails, what a sight they made!

As shadows grew long, stories filled the air,
The trees whispered jokes, with style and flair.
"Why did the leaf blush?" one asked with delight,
"Because it saw the tree strip in the moonlight!"

In this woodland realm, laughter rings true,
With critters and branches sharing what's new.
A funny old tale is forever retold,
In a forest of friendship, so warm, so bold.

Chronicle of a Timeworn Tree

Once stood a tree, with wisdom and age,
With stories woven in bark like a page.
He'd tell us of storms that rattled his frame,
Yet laughed at the lightning, saying, "I'm not lame!"

His branches are crooked, a sight to behold,
A home for a squirrel who's also quite old.
He claims he's the king of the woodland grand,
But lost to a rabbit in a race on the sand!

"Great tree, what's your secret?" the critters all plead,
He cackles and says, "Just plant yourself, and feed!
With sunshine and rains, and a sprinkle of cheer,
You'll grow every year, while drinking a beer!"

So gather around for the tree's funny verse,
Each line full of laughter, a woodland rehearse.
A chronicle rich, with jesters and glee,
In the heart of the forest, he's as wild as can be.

A Song for the Fallen Bough

Once a proud branch, swayed high on a vine,
Wished to be famous, for his dance divine.
He waved to the breeze, and he spun in delight,
Till a bird flew down and gave him a fright!

"Why are you swaying like you've lost your mind?
Just be still and let the sun shine!"
The branch replied, "I'm a performer, you see,
I'll shake off the leaves, and impress you with glee!"

But alas, one strong gust sent him tumbling down,
He landed with flair, then wore sticks as a crown.
He laughed at his fate, declared it a win,
"Now I'm the life of the ground, come join in!"

So here's to the bough that found joy in his fall,
A song of a branch who still dances for all,
With laughter and roots forever entwined,
In the heart of the forest, true joy you will find.

Rustling Pages of the Wild

In the pages of leaves, stories spin round,
Of critters and breezes, and fun to be found.
The rabbit writes tales with a quill made of grass,
While the snail publishes, slow but with sass.

The butterfly's words are like laughter in flight,
"Why don't we open a book club tonight?"
The hedgehog brought snacks, and they all took a seat,
As beetles recited their poems so sweet.

A squirrel shared gossip, with flair and a dash,
"Last night, I stole nuts, oh, what a mad stash!"
While the fox in the corner just snickered and grinned,
"Next time, little buddy, be less of a wind!"

So turn to the wild, where stories run free,
With laughter and friendship, just like a jubilee.
In rustling pages, let the wildness unfold,
Funny tales of the forest forever retold.

Gaze into the Graying Horizon

As I stand with my roots so deep,
I ponder the secrets that trees must keep.
The squirrels debate as they scurry around,
While I just stand here, firmly ground.

A bird lands on me, gives a cheeky squawk,
Strutting like he's the king of the block.
"Feathered fool," I chuckle with glee,
"Do you think you could ever grow quite like me?"

The wind whispers tales of the days gone by,
And I try not to laugh when the branches sigh.
"Do we age like cheese? Or fine wine, perhaps?"
I ponder as I watch the squirrels do laps.

But oh! To be silly is the best of all.
A tree can be wise, but still have a ball.
As I gaze into this graying affair,
I find joy in my roots, my foliage, and air.

Ink of Seasons on Weathered Bark

Each ring upon me tells a story or two,
Of storms I've conquered and sunshine I knew.
My bark bears the ink of nature's good cheer,
Yet kids with their nails, they come in near.

They carve their names, oh, what a sight!
"Here lies a tree, who's still in the fight!"
I grin at the antics, their giggles so bright,
While a squirrel jumps by, claiming he's right.

The winter's cold ink might make me shiver,
But come springtime, I'll dance and deliver.
Leaves flutter like pages upon a book,
Each rustle a story in very own nook.

So bring on the seasons, let them unfold,
With laughter and madness – remember, I'm bold!
For ink on my bark is the mark of great fun,
So carve if you must, my story's just begun.

A Lament for Lost Branches

Oh, the branches I've lost, they were quite the sight,
   Swinging high in the air, a true bird's delight.
   Now I stand, half-lopsided, a sight to behold,
   With stories of branches that dared to be bold.

   "Gone with the wind!" I'd holler and croak,
   While critters nearby would giggle and joke.
   "Did they fly to the moon? Or join in a band?"
The rumors keep swirling, like leaves in the land.

As the seasons change, I'll still wear my crown,
Though missing a branch, I won't frown or drown.
   For each loss I've faced is just part of the game,
   And I'll laugh at the past, that is how I stay tame.

   So here's to the branches, wherever they went,
May they find fun and mischief, I pray they repent.
   For with or without them, I carry their laugh,
   A whimsical tree, living life like a gaffe.

The Watcher of the Woodland Edge

At the edge of the woods, I stand ever so keen,
Watching all the critters, both silly and mean.
The rabbits are fussing, the deer take a glance,
While I chuckle inside at the wildlife's dance.

"Oh, my furry friends, what a crazy parade,
With high hops and dodges, your antics displayed!"
But out here on the edge, I keep my cool glare,
As a raccoon steels berries from out of thin air.

From dawn to dusk, I witness it all,
Birds singing off-key, and squirrels at a brawl.
"Go on, do your thing, make a peculiarity,"
I shout with delight, "that's the true quality!"

So come one, come all, to this lively show,
Where I'm just a watcher, but I steal the glow.
With laughter and humor right here on the fringe,
A tree stands tall, with branches that cringe.

Guardianship of the Grounded

In the shade of a leafy tent,
Squirrels chatter, their time well spent.
Hiding acorns, then losing the knack,
A forgotten stash – oh, what a whack!

Worms complain of the wormy plight,
Having a picnic deep in the night.
Roots argue over who's in the way,
While ants march on like they own the day.

The breeze tickles the branches high,
Even the leaves wave a cheeky goodbye.
Birds swoop down for a daring dive,
Life in the park – oh, it's quite alive!

With a creak and a groan, the trunk takes a stand,
Declaring it's king of this leafy land.
But with laughter and rustle, it starts to sway,
In this grounded kingdom, fun rules the day!

Stories Woven in Bark and Heart

Whispering tales in grooves and lines,
The bark tells secrets over apples and pines.
Every gnarled twist has a tale to spin,
Of picnics gone wild or the neighbor's grin.

A bird once claimed a branch as her throne,
"Stay out of my nest!" she squawked with a moan.
While an old spider spun webs in despair,
"I was here first, but nobody cares!"

The grass beneath chuckles, sways in delight,
As shadows dance on a warm summer night.
Squirrels trade tales of mischievous quests,
While evening descends with a soft, furry rest.

And thus in the bark, each line's a delight,
Stories ring true, even in flight.
The ground held snug, with giggles and mirth,
Nature's own laughter, the joy of the earth!

The Enduring Embrace of Green

In a hug of green that covers the floor,
Laughter bursts forth, who could ask for more?
The vines intertwine like gossiping friends,
Sharing wild tales that never quite ends.

The sun peeks in with a playful grin,
Chasing shadows like it wants to win.
Flowers chuckle as bees get too bold,
"Careful now, buddy, our nectar's not sold!"

Each rustling leaf holds a giggle or two,
As breezes blow whispers in emerald hue.
The dance of the branches, a playful affair,
Bringing a smile to everyone there.

So here's to the green, steadfast and bright,
With joy intertwined in every sunlight.
Though seasons may roll, fun's here to stay,
In this enduring embrace, come join the play!

Tales from the Trunk of Memories

Once a young sprout with a bold little dream,
Now a grand trunk with stories to beam.
Kids carved their names, a tattooed delight,
Reminders from summers that danced in the light.

"Do you remember," the trunk softly sighs,
"When we played hide-and-seek in disguise?"
The laughter of children, so vibrant and clear,
Fills up the ring where time disappears.

A squirrel named Nutty claims he's the best,
In acorn competitions that never find rest.
The trunk shakes with laughter, a thrum through the bark,

"Next time we'll see who can leap through the park!"

And so here they gather, through seasons and years,
Sharing their stories, their laughter, and tears.
In the heart of the trunk, a legacy grows,
Of cherished memories and the mirth that bestows.

Reverie of the Silent Watcher

In the still of the night, I spy a squirrel,
Chasing his tail, giving quite a twirl.
He leaps with grace, takes a dive and a tumble,
Then shakes off the leaves, oh what a humble!

From my sturdy roots, I laugh with delight,
At the antics of creatures under moonlight.
A wise old friend, this tree life I lead,
Serving up shade for all in their need.

With friends up above, I nod to the birds,
Who sing me sweet songs, just a few silly words.
They chatter and flap, a comical show,
While I stand unmoved—what a fine way to grow!

And so here I stand, as the seasons fly by,
A silent observer, while critters comply.
With laughter around, and sun shining bright,
Being a tree, well, it feels just right!

Echoing Through the Ages

Once there was a tree, who wanted to dance,
But his roots held him firm, oh what a chance!
He wiggled his leaves, gave a nod to the breeze,
While the rabbits hopped past, giggling with ease.

Centuries passed, yet still he would sway,
His boughs held a rhythm, in the funniest way.
The owls would hoot with a chuckle or two,
As his branches flailed 'round, feeling quite blue.

With squirrels all around, it became quite a mess,
Chasing their tails, always seeking finesse.
Each leap became laughter, each trip was a cheer,
As the forest erupted in giggles sincere.

Through the echoes of time, he learned to just grin,
Being serious? Well, where's the fun in?
So remember, dear friend, when life gets you stuck,
Just dance like a tree, and try out your luck!

Beneath the Grey Sky's Gaze

Beneath the grey sky, where rain likes to play,
A grumpy old tree had a rather rough day.
With raindrops like jokes, falling down from above,
He'd grumble and mumble, where's sunshine, my love?

Along came a crow, with a hat far too small,
"Why frown, dear old trunk? Just embrace it all!"
"While you stew in the storm, I'll dance in the drops,
And let's see who laughs as the laughter then tops!"

The tree had to chuckle, his bark echoed bright,
At the sight of that crow, what a hilarious sight!
So he swayed in the wind, and he joined in the fun,
Realizing now, he could shine without sun.

So when clouds come near, don't you ever dismay,
Just take a deep breath, and let laughter sway.
For life as a tree, though it may seem quite sad,
Is a comedy show, where being silly ain't bad!

Tapestry of Growth and Loss

Once a small acorn, nestled tight in the earth,
Dreamed of the day when he'd share his great worth.
Up he shot high, dreaming big, feeling grand,
Until a fierce storm took his hat off, unplanned.

He stood there uncovered, a crown made of leaves,
"I'm still pretty royal," he laughed as he breathes.
"Though I lost my top hat, new friends come my way,
With foxes and rabbits, we brighten the day!"

And through all the seasons, he learned how to cope,
In the tapestry woven with laughter and hope.
"Loss is a joke," he replied with a grin,
"We grow ever taller, let the fun times begin!"

So here's to the trees, with their hearts full of cheer,
Who dance in the wind, and don't quake out of fear.
Life is a circus, with ups and some downs,
But we laugh through it all, wearing joy as our crowns!

Hushed Tales of Twilight

In the shade where whispers grow,
Squirrels argue, tails in tow.
A crow caws loud, a toast to fleas,
While acorns plummet from the trees.

Chipmunks gather, party hats,
Joking 'bout their nutty stats.
Who won the race to stash a snack?
The tortoise claims, "I've got the knack!"

Rabbits hop with reckless grace,
While foxes strut, they own the place.
They twirl and spin, a wild affair,
But trip on roots, a sight so rare!

As dusk descends, the moon can't wait,
To join the fun with a glowing gait.
Beneath the trees, the laughter flows,
In twilight's grasp, the mischief grows.

The Resonance of Autumn's Breath

Leaves are crunching, oh what fun,
Dancing down, a quickened run.
A pumpkin rolls—what's that? A race!
The scarecrow twerks with a silly face.

Squirrels plotting in secret lairs,
Who can hoard the biggest pears?
"Let's throw acorns, start a feud!"
While nature laughs, it's clearly rude!

A rustling breeze, the branches sway,
Whispers of who's gone astray.
The cartoonish owls blink in delight,
Mocking the creatures that take flight.

With cocoa mugs and laughter bright,
The woods come alive, a silly sight.
Autumn giggles, dances about,
As twilight drops the curtain out.

Veins of Life Within the Earth

Roots entwine, a tangled mess,
"Excuse me!" grunts the tree in dress.
Worms parade; they've made a scene,
"Look at us! We're cozy, clean!"

Under soil, the funny chats,
Mice debate the pros and cons of hats.
"Should we wear leaves or tiny blooms?"
"Or just stick to our regular zooms?"

Frogs in the mud rehearse a play,
While toads croak lines in a bumbling way.
"Cast me as hero, don't read the script!"
"Stop hopping around, you'll get flipped!"

Earth's a stage, with laughter loud,
The acorns cheer, "Let's draw a crowd!"
And though they're rooted, they still find mirth,
In the lively chatter beneath the earth.

Fables of Solidity

Sturdy trunks with tales to share,
"Anyone seen my comb?" with flair.
The wind chuckles, knows the score,
While branches wave, they all adore.

Breezes carry giggles near,
"Don't look now, the grass is sheer!"
It tickles toes of passing bees,
Who buzz around like lost car keys.

Fables told in bark and leaf,
Of adventurers, full of belief.
"Remember when we crashed today?"
"Let's try again, hip-hip-hooray!"

And as the sun dips low and bright,
The woods erupt in endless light.
Solid stories spin in glee,
In the kingdom where roots roam free.

Echoes of Ancient Roots

In the garden where I stand,
My branches sway, it's quite a band.
Squirrels chatter, birds make a fuss,
I'm just here for the shade, no need to rush.

Whispers of the past, they creep,
A gnome's lost hat, a secret to keep.
Fungi dance, in their little hats,
I chuckle softly, as they sit like that.

Oh, the tales I could spin,
Of acorns that took it on the chin.
Lightning bolts that missed the mark,
I still stand tall, though once I was stark!

With roots to tickle and leaves to tease,
I host a party, if you please.
Let's raise a toast to all that's green,
To the laughter that sprouts in between!

Gnarled Wisdom in Solitude

In the quiet, I ponder all day,
Why do birds insist on their play?
With wisdom gnarled like my own bark,
I watch their antics, a giggling lark.

Old folks tell tales of how I've grown,
But I chuckle, they've seeds overblown.
For each weathering storm I proclaim,
I've still got roots, and I'm not to blame!

A passing beetle sought sage advice,
I told him, "Kid, don't roll that dice!"
But he shrugged it off, off he went,
Now he's the town's best pest-repellent!

So here I sit, alone but wise,
Watching the clouds and the silly flies.
Life is quirky, what do you think?
Let's lean back, and share a drink!

Seasons of the Silent Sentinel

Winter's chill brings squirrels' dread,
Wrapped in fluff, they dance instead.
While I stand firm like a statue in snow,
They throw snowballs, calling 'Let's go!'

Spring arrives with a floral show,
Blossoms bloom, but what do I know?
With bees buzzing like tiny cars,
I shake my leaves, and curse those jars!

Summer's heat, I'm a shady boss,
Sunbathers turn my trunk to gloss.
They lay beneath, in a sunny daze,
I think I'll drop some leaves as a prank that plays!

Autumn, oh my, the harvest mess,
Folks with baskets, who can guess?
They gather what falls, I watch with glee,
'Just keep the acorns!' I shout with a plea!

The Last Stand of a Titan

Once I was mighty, now I'm a joke,
Plants waltz around me like they're bespoke.
Yet here I am, with my gnarled old face,
Holding court in this woodland place.

They say I creak like an old man's chair,
But watch how I sway, still nothing to share!
The rabbits giggle, the critters enjoy,
While I stand strong, their leafy toy.

In storms I've rumbled, in sunlight I grin,
Oh, what a life for the king of skin!
With mossy robes and a mighty crown,
The last of the titans, you can't knock me down!

So let them laugh, let the stories unfurl,
For each ring in my trunk, there's a tale to swirl.
Hey there, fine friends, let's share in delight,
For even old trees can twirl in the night!

The Elder's Last Soliloquy

Once stood a tree, proud and tall,
With squirrels and birds who'd often call.
But time's cruel dance took all its hair,
Now it's just bark, but it doesn't care.

A twig fell off, 'Oh, what a fright!'
It thought it'd end up out of sight.
But kids made bows, and that gave a grin,
'If I can't be tall, I'll be great at sin!'

'Keep your acorns, I'm done with those!
I've traded my shade for some vibrant prose.
In stories told, I'll reign supreme,
As the funny ole tree who lived the dream!'

So here's to the roots, with antics so grand,
Making folks laugh, just as I planned.
For life's but a joke, so chuckle along,
As I sway with the breeze, singing my song.

Whispered Memories on the Wind

In whispers soft, the branches sway,
'Remember that storm? What a wild day!'
A poodle flew by, in a hasty go,
With a bark of surprise, like, 'Where's the show?'

The acorns fell like a shower of rain,
And broke a window, oh what a pain!
The owner then danced, cursing the trees,
While we just chuckled in the cool breeze.

Once a young fam, grinning with glee,
Played tag 'round my trunk, it tickled me.
But nothing tops the day they got stuck,
A laughable sight: their sheer, bad luck!

So gather 'round, let's share these tunes,
Of dancing dogs and wild afternoons.
For in every memory, laughter aligns,
In silly moments, we truly shine.

Beyond the Boughs: A Story Ends

Beyond the boughs, where tales get spun,
An old oak chuckles, 'Oh, this is fun!'
It swayed with the breeze, telling each tale,
Of a squirrel who thought he could take flight, but failed.

A raccoon in masks, quite theatrical too,
Came to mug a tree and say, 'How do you do?'
The oak just chuckled, 'I'm safe and sound,
But you've lost your job as the town's best clown!'

As days began to wane, and sunset fell,
It winked at the stars, 'Ah, all is well!'
For even in endings, there's laughter so sweet,
In the tales of the trees, our joy is complete.

So raise up a cheer for the stories we've found,
In whispers and giggles, my roots, they abound.
For life is a joke, and every tree knows,
We laugh at the follies that each day bestows.

Ashes of Autumn's Golden Crown

Golden leaves dance in their final bow,
'Hey, don't forget us!' they cheer from the bough.
While acorns giggle, rolling on the ground,
'We're the snacks of the season, so how 'bout a round?'

The breeze whispered secrets, teasing the trunks,
'Don't you just love all these playful punks?'
A badger just snorted, 'Why, what a show!
As I dig my den, I'll share tales, you know!'

Now, remember the day, the great frightful flop,
When a bear slipped on leaves and went for a drop?
With a thud and a snort, the forest erupted,
As tree limbs all shook, 'Who knew clumsiness erupted!'

So here's to the folly that each autumn brings,
With laughter and stories, our hearts take wings.
As long as trees whisper, we'll laugh without fear,
In the golden crown of each ending year.

A Farewell in the Fading Light

In the twilight, leaves take a bow,
Grinning at the sun, 'We're not done now!'
With a rustle, they're whispering jokes,
'Who needs the moon? We're the funniest folks!'

Branches wave goodbye with flair,
Twirling in wind, without a care.
As shadows stretch and day gets shy,
They tease the stars, 'Catch us if you try!'

The Watcher's Final Song

Under the sky, the old tree sways,
Telling tall tales in quirky ways.
'Last dance of leaves, don't be so sour,
We were here for the party, not power!'

With acorns falling like confetti bright,
Squirrels applaud from their lofty height.
'One more jig before we fade,
Who knew aging could feel like a parade?'

Surrendering to Starlit Nights

When night falls, the branches laugh,
Cracking jokes on their leafy staff.
'How do the stars keep their shine so clean?
They need a scrub from the night-time queen!'

As shadows dance in the moon's soft glow,
The wise old tree puts on a show.
'Why don't we float away with the breeze?
Flying high, just with ease, please!'

Gales that Grieve in Silence

Gales roaring past with a gusty cheer,
The sturdy one chuckles, 'I've seen it all, dear!'
With each sigh of wind, a tale takes flight,
'You think you're wild? Try my leaf-collected nights!'

As they whisper secrets, rustling for fun,
'Blow us away if you think you've won!'
The old tree just grins, with roots held tight,
For in every gust, there's a giggle of light!

Tales of a Weathered Canopy

Once I stood tall, a regal sight,
Now I'm a perch for squirrels that bite.
Birds drop their treasures, oh what a feat,
Now I wear acorns like fancy feet.

Beneath my boughs, the kids play around,
They climb and they swing, what joy they have found.
But when they get stuck, they holler and scream,
While I just laugh softly, a long, leafy dream.

The Age of the Sturdy Grain

Time crawls like snails, beneath my wide leaves,
Waiting for whispers, or so it believes.
Sunshine turns grumpy, clouds start to frown,
As I tell my jokes to the folks in town.

With roots like old tales and branches that sway,
I watch all the nonsense unfold every day.
I've seen centuries pass, full of cheer and of gloom,
Yet still, here I stand, in this infinite room.

Reflections of the Forgotten Seasons

Seasons come knocking, a comedic show,
Winter wears slippers, while summer's aglow.
Autumn's like grandma, with sweaters so bright,
Spring brings the flowers that tickle and bite.

I chuckle at squirrels, with acorns in tow,
Collecting their hoard, with yeti-like snow.
They bury them deep, or so they believe,
Only to find, it's just old rotting leaves!

Closing the Circle of Time

Each ring in my trunk tells a story bizarre,
Of gales and of giggles, and nuts in the jar.
I've seen lovers picnic and kids take a swing,
Only to leave with a songbird to sing.

I laugh at the seasons, each one has a role,
From frisky young buds to the wise, ancient coal.
When sunsets approach, I'll still crack a grin,
For every good moment's a reason to spin.

In the Shadow of the Towering Silence

In the shadow of a giant tree,
A squirrel knocked down a cup of tea.
It spilled and splashed, oh what a mess,
The birds just laughed, I must confess.

The tree stood tall, with regal grace,
Yet all around, a wild goose chase.
Frogs leaped high, with croaks of glee,
While bees were buzzing, oh so free.

A raccoon waltzed, with style and flair,
The tree just watched, with rooted stare.
Whispers of leaves, a chatter so bright,
"Who needs silence? Let's dance tonight!"

And so beneath that towering mass,
The woodland critters raised a glass.
A toast to chaos, loud and proud,
In the heart of nature, we're all avowed.

A Riddle in the Rustling Grass

In the tall grass, a riddle lay,
A frog declared, "I'm here to play!"
He hopped in circles, a puzzling sight,
While crickets chirped, from morning to night.

"What's green and loud, and loves to prance?"
The wise old owl offered a chance.
But all the frogs just leapt or croaked,
The more they guessed, the more they joked.

With every guess, the laughter grew,
A witty game, the sky so blue.
But who won what? Beneath the sun,
The grass stood still—riddles undone!

Yet with the dusk, they shimmied close,
Together they laughed, that's what they chose.
A riddle's charm won not by mind,
But in the joy that they all find.

The Solitary Echo of Existence

An echo bounded through the trees,
As leaves giggled in the teasing breeze.
A rabbit wondered, "What's with the sound?"
"Just a silly rumor going 'round!"

The wise old branch shook with a grin,
"It's just the world trying to fit in.
Why take things so terribly serious?
Life's a buffet—let's be curious!"

A butterfly flitted, with colors that danced,
"Maybe it's just all by chance!"
Laughter erupted, from critters of all kind,
In the echo of joy, they were entwined.

So in silence, they shared a secret song,
That sometimes echoes can lead you along.
And upon that note, they all took flight,
In the joyous arms of the fading light.

Beyond the Green Tapestry

Beyond the green, where laughter swells,
The snails have stories that no one tells.
They sip their tea and munch their leaves,
Plotting mischief no one believes.

A hedgehog snorted, "I'll join your fate!"
Said the snails, "First, let's clean the plate!"
With a dash of spice and a pinch of fun,
The leafy banquet had just begun.

As night descended, they heard a tune,
The fireflies swirled, dancing in the moon.
"Join us!" they flashed, in rhythm and rhyme,
Celebrating life, one spark at a time.

So gather, dear friend, in nature's grand spree,
In the heart of the wild, sip your tea.
For beyond the green, we're all intertwined,
In laughter and joy, the best we can find.

www.ingramcontent.com/pod-product-compliance
Lightning Source LLC
Chambersburg PA
CBHW071822160426
43209CB00003B/174